Obedience 101

"I Must Decrease"

By Michelle Langford

Dedication

This book is dedicated to my King forever, JESUS CHRIST. My BFF, the HOLY SPIRIT, and my GREAT ABBA, truly my inspiration for all things!

To my family: You are my heartbeat. Each of you bring a certain spice to my life it wouldn't be the same without.

To Howard, my husband of 30 years with whom this journey began when it was just a dream of mine to be able to do what I am doing today. You've given me such a rich perspective on life in Christ Jesus. You've taught me to stick to my guns in pursuit of my dreams. This journey with you has been one of love.

To My Children, Howard III, Caleb, Isaiah, Noah, and Zoe, each of you have brought me so much joy and so much material about which to write. You've pushed me in ways that only a mother could understand. I have so much hope and confidence in who God has called and ordained each of you to be. I love you for being you.

To My Mom and Dad, we've really pushed the envelope this year. I've seen life from an entirely different perspective because of you. Mommy, thank you for my early years. Daddy, thank you for my latter years. The best is still yet to come for us all.

To My Ride or Die, Cheryll Perry, you are by far the best big sister anyone could have. To all of my family members, thank you.

Thank you, to my Pastor, Corey K. McPherson Sr., who brought the message of obedience home to me. I am eternally grateful. First Lady, and New Willow Grove Church Family, I cannot possibly repay what I have gained as a result of our fellowship together. I appreciate what you have poured into me.

Introduction

In order to fully digest the gift, the instruction, the lesson in this book you must have a willing heart and give God permission and free reign to interrupt your life. If allowed, the Holy Spirit will disturb your plans and agenda in order to get the full profit and benefit from the gifts, talents, and purpose that He invested in you. He will do it if you're willing.

Most of us declare our allegiance to God, but we have far too many priorities ahead of Him. That will change when you go through this book if you're open to it. Your biggest challenge to the full benefit of the book is what you already know. You must be willing to unlearn the things that may be staples in your Christian theology and practice in order to receive the revelation of Obedience. This book removes all of the inhibitions that keep the body of Christ in a constant state of having a form of godliness, but denying the power thereof.

If you're willing God will set an appointment on His calendar to engage in the writings of this book with you.

Table of Contents

Obedience is God's Language

Watching my five and six-year old boys wrestle in the aisles during morning service was a nightmare that seemed to be a nice fit for the old saying "boys will be boys." My husband was on the drums and I couldn't muster up another ounce of energy to pull them in line. As bad as it seemed, all I could do was look at my friends and laugh who were also laughing because they too had small children and understood what I was going through. Unlike mothers from previous generations, I didn't have a look that could bring them in line. My mother had a look, but it wasn't used very often so I never became overly familiar with it. My grandmother had a look that I saw almost every time I saw her. She was a serious woman with a beautiful smile, but I knew when she meant business.

Somehow the ball got dropped from my grandmother's generation to my mother's. I think that having such harsh things happen to her when she was a child, my mother must have made up in her mind that she would never treat her children that way. She never did. My sister and I got a spanking once when we were younger for not cleaning the house, but never really any other time until I became a teenager. My teenage years were riddled with belt crackers in the garage after getting caught sneaking in the window, lying about where I was, or disobeying something that I was or was not supposed to do. They say a hard head makes a soft behind and it did. By the time I was nineteen years old, in my mind, I'd lived a full life and was ready to settle down and learn something different, obedience.

I've always been a good student when I've applied myself to learning. Yet, my high school years wreaked of averageness. College at 18 years old was a bust. My first try ended with a financial aid suspension because I hadn't passed enough classes to warrant the government giving me more money to attend the same school. Additionally, I'd left a balance in the student accounts office that prevented me from reregistering for any more semesters until the balance was paid in full. Longing so deeply for a better life, over the five years between twenty years old, when I flunked out, and twenty-five years old, as a literally poor and desperate housewife, I prayed diligently for the Lord to please allow me to finish my college education. I didn't know what I would do with the education. I just wanted to prove to myself that I could do it. Somehow, I knew that if God gave me another chance, I would master the art of being a good student. I would take advantage of the opportunity given to develop the disciplinary habits needed to advance in the act of learning something new. It doesn't matter if you're three, thirty-three, or sixty-six, it's never too late to become a student in God's classroom.

Obedience is what we learn first. It's the first lesson on day one. In most classrooms, from kindergarten through secondary school, a great educator will take time to develop a rapport with the student's both individually and as a whole. Quite to the contrary, in college many professors don't care about a rapport. They're there to execute. It's solely the student's responsibility to latch on to their style of teaching. I've taken college courses of difficult subject matter with professors who had a very thick accent. Over time, I've learned that that was a recipe for disaster in the classroom. The subject without the teacher's accent would have been difficult alone. Language without obstructions is essential to grasping any material or message that is being conveyed. As a quick study, I learned a few things that were necessary for success in my first years of college: never take an 8 a.m. class, assess the wiggle room of each professor for late assignments and nonsense, and drop the class immediately if you can't grasp teaching style or language of your professor. The rise and fall of great teachers hinges on their ability to communicate and connect with their students. A large part of that comes down to language.

There are models and educational programs for learning another language through what is called immersion. Immersion is a term that you may be familiar with when it comes to baptisms.

Some segments of the Christian faith think that sprinkling water on a baptismal candidate is okay, while others believe as I do, that immersion is the mandate for baptism. Immersion entails being plunged into the water so that the whole person is completely covered and there is no room for that pinky toe to be uncovered. In learning a second language, the 50/50 model of learning allows the students to be immersed into the language for half of their school day while being taught in their native language the other half of the day. This forces the students for at least half of their day to become one with the language.

Our God is one of immersion when it comes to obedience. He plunges us into the full expectation of following Him without any necessity to turn back. Obedience is like the language of God. Until you learn the basic rules of the language, it's hard to teach you anything else; no math, no science, no social studies. Learning the basic language first is your way of communicating to God that you understand what He said. What is beautiful about God is that He equips us with and interpreter, the Holy Spirit. The Holy Spirit guides us step by step into how to walk in obedience to the Father. We never have a need to refer to our old language. Therefore, we must develop a dependency on the Holy Spirit. In teaching a second language, it's often a benefit for the teacher to not know the native language of the person that they're teaching. This is true because if forces the learner to adapt to communicating in the language that is being taught.

Yes, obedience is an act of your will, but to God it translates into understanding. When you obey God, you are conveying the message that there are some things about Him and His role in your life that you understand. It also translates into love. Jesus said in John 14:15 "If you love me, keep my commandments." It was vital that disciples understand that obedience would translate into love because their assignment to evangelize the rest of the world would pivot on obedience. If the Father love the world and gave His son, and the Son loved the world that He gave His life, that same love would need to be the driving force behind reaching the nations. They needed to understand that just as Jesus kept the Father's commands, they should keep His commands.

There was no room for ambiguous messaging when the fate of the world was at stake. By the same token, our messaging to the world concerning Christ must be clear. We have been charged to convey the memorandum of God's love and redemption to every nation across the globe. Obedience is our language for doing that. Anything less is unclear and confusing.

At twenty-five years old, as soon as I learned that I was pregnant with my first son, I began to talk and read scriptures to him. I wanted him to understand that from the very first moment that I knew he was there that I loved him. I knew that he would be coming into a world with tremendous challenges so I had to make it clear before he got here that he was loved. If anything ever left him feeling unloved, I wanted it branded into his core from the beginning that he was loved beyond his current circumstance. Like I did, many parents begin to communicate with their children in a teachable language in order to establish boundaries for behavior and conduct.

Having a hearing-impaired child pushes parents even further with communication challenges that must be bridged in some way. Sign language for most parents of deaf children serves that purpose. In that same way, we being both spiritually deaf and blind, God communicated His love for us through the gift of His son. The son communicated His love for both the Father and us by His obedience to the Father. Therefore, obedience established before the foundation of the world, has been the uterus in which our relationship with God is forged.

Like most college freshmen, I learned that my four-year journey would begin with the one hundred series of courses. The one hundreds are foundational for all other classes. Fundamentals from high school Math, English, and the Sciences, regurgitated through these courses, serve as building blocks for our complex progressions in higher education. Likewise, Obedience 101 locks down the basic knowledge for faithful pursuits in Christianity. Without this simple building block, nothing else makes spiritual sense.

The first and principle rule of life in Christ Jesus stems out of Jesus' conversation with his disciples in Luke Chapter 9. He asks his disciples "Whom do men say that I am?" Peter declares Him to be the Christ, the son of the living God. Jesus says for them to tell no man. He goes on to share with them that He would suffer many things. Afterwards, He staples Obedience Rule #1 in their mental catalogues of the crucifixion chronicles. He says, *"If any man will come after me, let him deny himself, and take up his cross daily, and follow me."* It is impossible to disobey this rule and remain in compliance with the life of Jesus Christ. I said IMPOSSIBLE. Consequently, this book of obedience is about the death process, its real-time look, and what it means for you and I.

He Knows My Name

Hebrews 5:8
Though he were a Son, yet learned he obedience by the things which he suffered;

When I saw Him, I knew that I wasn't ready. On Thursday March 14, 2019, a light as bright as anything that I've ever seen shined in my face as I traveled home from work. My husband Howard had picked me up. I was in the passenger seat of our Jeep Cherokee on the way to pick up our oldest son Howard III when I had an experience very similar to that which the Apostle Paul described in the book of Acts.

Acts 9:3
3 And as he journeyed, he came near Damascus: and suddenly there shined round about him a light from heaven:
4 And he fell to the earth, and heard a voice saying unto him, Saul, Saul, why persecutest thou me?
5 And he said, Who art thou, Lord? And the Lord said, I am Jesus whom thou persecutest: it is hard for thee to kick against the pricks.

6 *And he trembling and astonished said, Lord, what wilt thou have me to do? And the Lord said unto him, Arise, and go into the city, and it shall be told thee what thou must do.*

Although I knew that I was still in my seat, my spirit had been lifted to another realm. Seemingly caught between heaven and earth, suspended within the bright light with its' beautiful gold ornamentation, I was being summonsed. I had an appointment with God that I wasn't aware of, but He wasn't willing to miss. I couldn't tell if it was the hem of His garment or what I was seeing. What was I seeing? Remarkable, it was just the brightest, purest light I'd ever seen. There are no words in our language that I could use to adequately give you the sense of what I felt in that moment. I understand now why He said that no man can see Him and live. It was as if the brightness of His glory would consume me and I would die. My heart was faint. It was literally indescribably breathtaking. A full blown, unharnessed sense of fear came over me. It had broken away from the measured tremble that had accompanied me throughout that day.

Earlier in the day, I'd called my sister Cheryll at about 2 o'clock that afternoon while on my lunch break at work. I'd told her that I could feel something in the air. Looking back, I can only fathom that the Lord had been following me, hovering over me, overshadowing me the whole day. The thought of it still terrifies me today. What I'd been feeling earlier in the day was the close proximity of the glory of His presence. The inseparable awe shackled to His magnificent splendor humbled me. I was bewildered with why He would show up to me.

Although the whole encounter lasted only minutes, it seemed like an eternity. In the terror of that moment, I began to reason in my heart and mind "What is the nature of this encounter?" The remarkable exchange between my creator and I was far beyond anything that I'd awakened thinking would happen to me on that day. I immediately began to question, "Lord, what is this? Am I going to die?" In the presence of the Lord, you know that you're encountering the source of your next breath. While He did not verbally answer "Yes" or "No", I understood that He wanted me to know that if He wanted to, He could suspend my breath. I measured my words.

I knew that I wasn't prepared to go. I could sense His displeasure with me. I hadn't done the things that He'd told me to do. I thought that I had so much more time. I couldn't understand why He was there. I knew that I was saved, so why the displeasure? My lack of obedience to Him was immediately my thought. I felt like the wicked and lazy servant spoken of in the bible. I knew that He'd given me a plethora of talents, but what was I doing with them? I was moving at my own pace. I felt like I had time, so the urgency to obey Him was not there. Instantly, I understood that I and most the people that I knew had misunderstood what He would be looking for when He returned. Somehow my definition of saved didn't seem to match His. How was that possible?!

Our acceptance of Jesus Christ into our hearts is one aspect of our salvation, but our daily obedience to Him impacts the completion of the work. Yes, Jesus died for us, but the scripture says that we are saved by grace through faith. Additionally, James 12:17 says "faith also if it does not have works, is dead." The grace for salvation was furnished in the death, burial, and resurrection of Christ. Most of us received the grace to save us from our sins, but not to walk out the plan of God for our lives.

When we said the sinner's prayer and asked Jesus to forgive us of our sins, we received the grace for our death completed in His death. When we walk away from the old life that we used to live, we acknowledge and receive the grace for our burial completed in His burial. Likewise, there must also be resurrection life in our lives in order for the completed work of Christ to be fulfilled in us. That resurrection life is walked out each day through obedience to Him just as He walked in obedience to His Father.

Paul pens it this way in Philippians 2:12-13 "Wherefore, my beloved, as ye have always obeyed, not as in my presence only, but now much more in my absence, work out your own salvation with fear and trembling. For it is God which worketh in you both to will and to do of his good pleasure." If our works were not important to our salvation, why would the apostle tell us to "work out our own salvation with fear and trembling?" What is there to fear and tremble about if Jesus did all of the work. Actually, He did do all of the work, but since we are dead, and our life is hidden with Christ in God, then were not actually doing the work, He is. Again, he says it is God who works in us both to will and to do His good pleasure.

Let's look at the wicked and lazy servant that I spoke of earlier for further clarification.

13 *Watch therefore, for ye know neither the day nor the hour*
wherein the Son of man cometh.
14 *For the kingdom of heaven is as a man travelling into a far*
country, who called his own servants, and delivered unto them
his goods.
15 *And unto one he gave five talents, to another two, and to*
another one; to every man according to his several ability; and
straightway took his journey.
16 *Then he that had received the five talents went and traded with*
the same, and made them other five talents.
17 *And likewise he that had received two, he also gained other*
two.
18 *But he that had received one went and digged in the earth, and*
hid his lord's money.
19 *After a long time the lord of those servants cometh, and*
reckoneth with them.
20 *And so he that had received five talents came and brought*
other five talents, saying, Lord, thou deliveredst unto me five
talents: behold, I have gained beside them five talents more.
21 *His lord said unto him, Well done, thou good and faithful*
servant: thou hast been faithful over a few things, I will make
thee ruler over many things: enter thou into the joy of thy lord.

[22] He also that had received two talents came and said, Lord, thou deliveredst unto me two talents: behold, I have gained two other talents beside them.
[23] His lord said unto him, Well done, good and faithful servant; thou hast been faithful over a few things, I will make thee ruler over many things: enter thou into the joy of thy lord.
[24] Then he which had received the one talent came and said, Lord, I knew thee that thou art an hard man, reaping where thou hast not sown, and gathering where thou hast not strawed:
[25] And I was afraid, and went and hid thy talent in the earth: lo, there thou hast that is thine.
[26] His lord answered and said unto him, Thou wicked and slothful servant, thou knewest that I reap where I sowed not, and gather where I have not strawed:
[27] Thou oughtest therefore to have put my money to the exchangers, and then at my coming I should have received mine own with usury.
[28] Take therefore the talent from him, and give it unto him which hath ten talents.
[29] For unto every one that hath shall be given, and he shall have abundance: but from him that hath not shall be taken away even that which he hath.
[30] And cast ye the unprofitable servant into outer darkness: there shall be weeping and gnashing of teeth.

Just like this servant, I have so often had my reasons for not doing the work that He asked me to do. Most of them centered around the reasoning for His command coupled with the lack of value attributed to God's ability to use me. Our proclivities and personality quirks can be major hinderances to the movement of God in our lives. I'm a planner by nature and I've often used the lack of time to prepare as my reason for not following through with God's instructions. God moves on a dime, on short notice sometimes. We have to be prepared to move with Him.

I didn't like feeling like I would be judged by the religious judges who say "You're doing too much." People always have an opinion about what you should be doing when they're not doing anything themselves. I wanted to avoid that kind of criticism so I didn't do the things that I was led to do. I've also held in my heart the thought process that says that I don't want to do anything that God hasn't led me to do. This has been another reason to just fall back and do nothing. However, that sounds like what the wicked and lazy servant said. He said to his master that I know that you are a hard man and that you reap where you do not sow, so I did nothing. He's saying, "Jesus I didn't want to be judged harshly by you for taking a wrong turn or missing one of your cues so I didn't launch out in obedience. "It's this kind of passive reasoning that is and affront to obedience.

Our job is to be available. Our attitude is to be willing. God's commands often require us to step out of the box of our comfort zones. Most of us don't fully process what that will look like in everyday service to Him. We have a prescribed set of services that we render to the Lord like attending 5a.m prayer, teaching bible study to the teens, attending Sunday Morning worship service, or going to the nursing homes when it is our week as ministers to perform that duty of the church. This list of services gives us a warm and fuzzy feeling of accomplishment in service to the Lord. However, God requires us to be attentive to His promptings every minute of every day. We should be on standby for minute by minute instructions because every moment in His kingdom counts.

Like a deep sleep interrupted by the violent shaking of the bed to awaken me, I was terrified! Lingering in the bright light on March 14th, I thought about my daughter and my family. In my mind, I knew that she needed me the most. Internally, I desperately pleaded for more time. Before I knew it, I gently blurted out the words, "I will live and not die!" At that moment, His presence lifted. I was visibly shaken. Even at that moment, in *the* worst-case scenario for me, He honored His word. I can only conceive that the Holy Spirit, my valuable helper, brought that scripture up out of my belly because He knew that I had more work to do. He knew that the Lord would honor it. He knew that I had to share this word with you.

Over the next few days and weeks the humbling effect of it all bowled me over in a fetal position on my bed or on my hands and knees rocking back and forth. The clarity of how great He is was inescapable. I couldn't hide from it or pretend that I didn't know. He'd decided that it was the time of *my* visitation, (Luke 19:44). I was bound from that day forward to be the full expression of His glory. Whatever that meant for me; Michelle was irrelevant. Whatever praise was required from me, I was compelled to give it. Never again would I shrink from the light or hold back.

That was the exchange between God and I, but there was so much more that happened in that encounter that I want to share with you in this book. We're told in 1 Corinthians 13:12 "For now we see through a glass, darkly; but then face to face: now I know in part; but then shall I know even as also I am known." Although I don't still fully "*know*" Him, I know Him in a much better way today; and much better than I ever thought that I could on this earth.

All kinds of scriptures become real to you when the Lord reveals Himself in them. Though I know that the scripture talks about the good shepherd leaving the ninety-nine to search for the one, I never dreamed that He loved me enough to physically come and see about me. I was that one.

I seem to have a knack for miscalculating the measure of His love for me. Similarly, in the days before I got saved in 1989, I made a request of God that again He fully met. Living without the light of Jesus Christ shining in my heart, in utter darkness, I said to Him "God, I know that you sent Jesus to die on the cross for the world, but if you *really* love *me* can you send me a personal invitation? I really don't know what I was expecting, but within the next few days, as real any personal encounter, as I slept in my bed one night, I dreamed of riding down the highway when Jesus appeared in the sky. My sister and I were riding in her old beat up forest green Chevy Malibu when she suddenly ascended into the air to meet Him.

Completely devastated that I was left in the car as they disappeared, I awakened with a trembling in the depths of my soul that I'd never experienced before. It was with that same tremble that I spent the next three or four days of that year wrapped in a fetal position in my bed crying, sobbing, and repenting before the Lord for how desperately I had missed Him. I could literally feel the tug of war back and forth in my soul. I knew that I was in the midst of an eternal transaction; and I was terrified. I just kept crying! Finally, I asked the Lord Jesus to come into my heart and save me.

Eternal Transactions

The eternal transactions spoken of should not be overlooked or undervalued. God the Father, our Abba, loves His son, the Word of God. However, He also loved us so much that He would give the blood of His son in exchange for our lives. The great revelation in this entire exchange is the value of the blood of Jesus. This blood has the ability to redeem a soul from hell and damnation. At that moment of our decision, there has already been a negotiation for the redemption of our lives. The Father has been in counsel with us over the terms of the contract. He's shared with us the great benefit to us of receiving the Lord Jesus Christ into our hearts. The only thing left for us to do is to agree, say "Yes". Upon our agreement, He's at the counter of eternal exchange saying "Give me my baby back!" with the blood on site for the redemption of our lives.

Matthew 18:12.

*"How think ye? If a man have an hundred sheep, and one of them be gone astray, doth he not leave the ninety and nine, and goeth into the mountains, and seeketh that which is gone astray? **13**And if so be that he find it, verily I say unto you, he rejoiceth more of that sheep, than of the ninety and nine which went not astray. **14**Even so it is not the will of your Father which is in heaven, that one of these little ones should perish.*

Again, on that day, I was that one.

Wait on the Lord

"Even the youth shall faint and be weary, and the young men shall utterly fall: But they that wait upon the Lord shall renew their strength; they shall mount up with wings as eagles; they shall run, and not be weary; and they shall walk, and not faint."

I can't emphasize the weight of this particular scripture enough. Almost thirty years ago at the beginning of my walk with God, the Lord began to speak this word to my spirit. I didn't grasp it in its' fullness back then because the context in which I'd heard this word preached was always relative to waiting on God to fix a situation. I might have related it to a bill that I was waiting for God to pay, a check coming in the mail, or the baby that I had longed to have. It was never in the context of waiting in the presence of the Lord until the glory of God showed up. When the Lord presented it to me after His first appearance, that's the context in which He revealed it.

The first thing that I learned to do in obedience after my encounter with Jesus was to wait in His presence. We're all very familiar with Isaiah 40:30-31 "Even the youth shall faint and be weary, and the young men shall utterly fall: But they that wait upon the Lord shall renew their strength; they shall mount up with wings as eagles; they shall run, and not be weary; and they shall walk, and not faint." About a month after my encounter I had a dream in which the Lord guided me to the meaning of the scripture. In the dream I was in a foreign country which I won't name, but the color royal blue was very prominent in the dream. I was flying through the sky and came to land on the ground at the opening of the dream. Once I was on the ground, a woman beckoned me to come over to her. She pointed to a dresser drawer of some sort and said "Over here we have the mark of the beast." I then heard the voice of the Lord say "You've fallen behind. You're going to need the Holy Spirit to make your departure on time." At that moment I took off again into the air with a sense of urgency to catch up with the group that I was traveling with.

From that point, I knew that the Holy Spirit had to become my new BFF. I listened to hours and hours of teaching about the person of the Holy Spirit. I would fall asleep with Benny Hinn's book "Good Morning Holy Spirit" playing through my Alexa speaker. I began to listen to his teachings about waiting on the Lord. The presence of the Lord, the ministry of the Holy Spirit, and my attention to His promptings were all peaked. Holy Spirit shared with me so many scriptures to guide my priorities. In one of the Benny Hinn teachings there was even mention of falling behind and needing to catch up (like the words in my dream) stating that when you don't spend time waiting in His presence you miss His impartation into your spirit for that day. If you miss too many days, you could easily fall behind and begin to lose ground so that it may take several days to recover what you've lost. When the Lord needed me, His instruction was for me to be available. Here's what He said:

Matthew 22:37-38
37 *Jesus said unto him, Thou shalt love the Lord thy God with all thy heart, and with all thy soul, and with all thy mind.*
38 *This is the first and great commandment.*

Luke 14:26
"If any man come to me, and hate not his father, and mother, wife, and children, and brethren, and sisters, yea, and his own life also, he cannot be my disciple."

John 21:15
15 *So when they had dined, Jesus saith to Simon Peter, Simon, son of Jonas, lovest thou me more than these? He saith unto him,*

Yea, Lord; thou knowest that I love thee. He saith unto him, Feed my lambs.
[16] *He saith to him again the second time, Simon, son of Jonas, lovest thou me? He saith unto him, Yea, Lord; thou knowest that I love thee. He saith unto him, Feed my sheep.*
[17] *He saith unto him the third time, Simon, son of Jonas, lovest thou me? Peter was grieved because he said unto him the third time, Lovest thou me? And he said unto him, Lord, thou knowest all things; thou knowest that I love thee. Jesus saith unto him, Feed my sheep.*

The Lord makes it very clear in scripture that He should be our first priority. I'm stating that because waiting on the Lord takes time. Most of us don't think that we have time to wait on the Him in the way that He has prescribed us to. In order to obey the instruction to wait on the Lord, there is a reverence for His person, His place in your life, and His will that is needed to follow through. Our presumptuous movement without His instruction can leave us in a precarious place. I remember spending hours just basking in His presence. I wasn't doing anything necessarily, simply making myself available to Him and making sure that He understood that I was at His disposal.

The practical application of it was tested in July of 2019. My mother was overcome by an illness that had rendered her bedridden. She spent a few days in the hospital, but then she was transferred to a rehabilitation facility. There were so many ducks to get in a row with the rehabilitation facility that it was consuming my entire day sometimes. It was critical though so I had to do it. I had to stay engaged every day because there was also so much other family trauma that was underway that not being available seemed unthinkable. My parents being in their seventies were not familiar with all of the loopholes that had to be closed to make sure that the insurance companies covered my mother's care. There was a daily breakdown of something in their situation. Leaving them to handle it alone just seemed cruel and unthinkable.

Nevertheless, I'd been asked to preached at my church and I knew that I needed time with the Lord. I had just personally come out of a series of deliverances so I could not just brush God off as if I just knew that He would be with me in that preaching moment. I wanted to hear what He had to say. I wanted to know what He wanted me to share with His people. I could feel Him pulling me into "quarantine". This was prior to our 2020 pandemic wherein the whole world was shut up into quarantine. I even used the word "quarantine" when describing this season of what I could feel God calling me to with my husband. I told my husband that it's like God wants me in quarantine. This seemed to me to be for the purpose of preparation for this preaching event.

The timeframe that the Lord was pulling me away for seemed unusual and intrusive on my everyday life, but I couldn't say 'No." How could I? So, for a period of about two weeks I spent every day in the presence of the Lord in pursuit of His heart and His will. God even shared the scripture with me that says, "He that loveth father or mother more than me is not worthy of me: and he that loveth son or daughter more than me is not worthy of me." (*Matthew 10:37 KJV*) He was essentially saying that His assignment for me at that moment was the group of people to whom I would be preaching His word. That assignment had to supersede everything else in terms of importance. It had to be first on my priority list. I had to trust that if I devoted myself to Him in this way, He would take care of my parents. That goes back to the question that Jesus asked Peter, "Do you love me more than these", then "Feed my sheep."

This is the practical application of waiting on the Lord and obedience. This obedience paid a great dividend with my mother which I will share with you in a later chapter.

Willing

Isaiah 1:19-20 King James Version (KJV)
[19] If ye be willing and obedient, ye shall eat the good of the land:
[20] But if ye refuse and rebel, ye shall be devoured with the sword: for the mouth of the Lord hath spoken it.

I thought that as long as I was obedient then the Lord would find my service acceptable. A year into my awakening the Lord began to deal with me about my willingness to follow His plan. Willingness is probably the most ardent place of rebuttal that God had to wrestle with me over. It's not that I didn't love God. It's that "I" was standing in my own way of being obedient. I'd accepted the calling to preach the gospel ten years after He called me because I don't like to be the focal point of any event. I didn't want to stand in front of people and convey to them the message of the Lord. It was the standing in front of people that was hindering me. The entire thought process of depending on God to give me the words to say while seventy-five to one hundred people stare at me was not on my bucket list. As a natural introvert, the thought of it was horrifying.

I remember the first time that I was asked to pray in front of our large church congregation. During Sunday School, I was in the bathroom with butterflies standing over the toilet ready to be sick. This problem persisted for me so badly in my younger years of high school that when it was my day to go to the front of the class to perform CPR on a dummy while the entire class watched me, I faked sick to stay home from school. I ended up performing CPR on the dummy in the hallway on the next day without the stares of my classmates who were moving on with the next lesson.

You can't fake sick with God. He forces us to confront the horrors that terrify us by running towards them. With as many things as He'd brought me through, I hadn't figured out yet that if I was willing He would give me the grace to perform His will. He can do anything. I hadn't paired His ability to do anything with my ability to be used by Him. While on many fronts, I can be fearless, like when it comes to issues that concern my children. Yet, when it comes to me subjecting myself to the judgment and abuse of others, I'm less likely to sign up for a role. Honestly, most of the things that God calls us to do will cause us to be judged by other people. It comes with the territory. He gives us a plethora of scriptures to help us to mentally arm ourselves. This is an area where a strong mind is needed. This is why the Apostle Paul said to Timothy in 2 Timothy 1:7 "God has not given to us the spirit of fear, but of power, love, and a sound mind." Timothy was a young pastor who was trying to lead a church of people older than himself. The intimidation of coming against the tradition of Judaism had to be daunting for the young fellow. Nevertheless, he was encouraged not to allow his gift to lie dormant, but to stir it up.

If we continue to look at people for their approval, we will NEVER complete the will of God. There is always going to be opposition to your completion of God's requests. We have to venture past people and their opinions and focus on the one who has the crown. God orchestrates our lives to fulfill His covenant agreement with us. Our obedience is key to that end. We're often positioned in the presence of people and in particular places for the purpose of divine destiny. If we never challenge ourselves to move outside of what is traditional, move outside of man's rules and regulations, and move outside of mental thought patterns that keep us locked in places of averageness and mediocrity, we may never complete the assignment for which we were sent to the earth in the first place.

There are numerous stories of great warriors in the bible who ran towards their destiny like David did Goliath, but there are just as many, if not more stories of frightened and intimidated vessels who followed God's plan with a little coaxing. One of my favorite responses to God's call is that of Moses most likely because my answer was similar to that of Moses. From Moses' response to God, it sounded like this was the last thing that Moses wanted to do, listen:

Exodus 3:10-11 *[10] Come now therefore, and I will send thee unto Pharaoh, that thou mayest bring forth my people the children of Israel out of Egypt.*
[11] And Moses said unto God, Who am I, that I should go unto Pharaoh, and that I should bring forth the children of Israel out of Egypt?

Exodus 4:1

And Moses answered and said, But, behold, they will not believe me, nor hearken unto my voice: for they will say, The Lord hath not appeared unto thee.

[10] And Moses said unto the Lord, O my Lord, I am not eloquent, neither heretofore, nor since thou hast spoken unto thy servant: but I am slow of speech, and of a slow tongue.
[14] And the anger of the Lord was kindled against Moses, and he said, Is not Aaron the Levite thy brother? I know that he can speak well. And also, behold, he cometh forth to meet thee: and when he seeth thee, he will be glad in his heart.
[15] And thou shalt speak unto him, and put words in his mouth: and I will be with thy mouth, and with his mouth, and will teach you what ye shall do.
[16] And he shall be thy spokesman unto the people: and he shall be, even he shall be to thee instead of a mouth, and thou shalt be to him instead of God.

Moses first response was to question his own identity as it relates to fulfilling God's calling on his life. Then Moses was leery of the response that he would receive from the Israelites. For his final argument, Moses brought up his handicap and insecurity. These are all responses that many of us tend to have when it comes to following God's plan. Just like Moses, I didn't feel worthy to carry the gospel of Jesus Christ. I knew that I'd lived a ratchet life and felt like a preacher needed to be someone who'd live a clean life. Even though I was already saved, I still had a hard time embracing the fullness of the work of Christ in my life. I also thought that people would question whether or not God had spoken to me. I had a strong pull in the direction of preaching. God showed himself on many occasions when I stood up to speak, but I was still unsure. He's told me in a number of ways that He needed me to open my mouth, but I was still afraid. Lastly, just like Moses, I shared with God every insecurity that I had which would keep me from being a good preacher. Nevertheless, His call on my life remained sure as it has on yours as well.

A Lesson in Dying, Always Remember Jesus

(The Death Process)

In thirty years of salvation, no one had adequately explained what Jesus meant when He said, take up your cross and follow me. It was never fully revealed what the statement, except a grain of corn falls to the ground and dies, it abides alone meant. Better yet, whosoever saves his life will lose it, but whoever gives it up for my sake will have eternal life was not elaborated upon in a way that detailed the necessity to change all of the things that made me *me*. The idiosyncratic ones, you know? Although, Jesus did make numerous references to indicate that He fully expects us to die. Dying is not a topic that anyone readily jumps into because we associate it with the morbid reality of our earthly ending.

What Jesus is talking about in these verses is the death to our own will and personal proclivities as He died to His will in the Garden of Gethsemane. The scriptures tell us that our lives are not our own. They were purchased with a price. The only way to get the redemptive value of the life that was purchased is if the "owner" of that life willfully yields it to the redemption. While Jesus completed the "legal" exchange of His life for ours on the cross in the spirit realm, in the physical fleshly realm we must also agree to surrender our lives to Him. Our life consists of more than a physical body. We are a spirit. We have a soul. We live in a body. All three components of spirit, soul, and body must yield in agreement to the will of Jesus Christ being walked out every day in our flesh.

While gaining this understanding from the Lord, I spent numerous hours considering and meditating on the death of Jesus Christ. I wanted to do my best to fully understand what He went through on the cross. Even when I think of it today, it makes me cry to know that He endured so much just for me. I've considered the mental anguish that He went through knowing what the days of His passion would entail. At each stage, from the last supper, to the garden, to the judgment halls, to the trials, then to sentencing, I walk fully engulfed in understanding His process. I thought about the hours upon hours of Him hanging there on the cross from 9am to 3pm our time, in excruciating pain, knowing that at any moment He could have come down. What kind of mental preparation does it take to be that committed to a purpose like that? As He hung there with the nails digging larger and larger holes through His flesh, was He still in worship mode as He expects us to be? Those are the things that I live my life considering now.

I think about what Mary went through, considering the fullness of the crucifixion in contrast and coincidence with what we go through. There had to be something exceptionally powerful that Mary was equipped with in order to be able to watch them do that to her son. From a mother's perspective, it's a virtual impossibility to watch as your son is crucified for wrongs that He didn't commit without a powerful anointing of grace to endure a process. The mental preparation that she also must have had to have is untold. This gives us a sense of the psychological groundwork that had to be laid in order for the crucifixion to go forth as it did. We are not told of Mary beating up the guards or being dragged off of the scene because of her uncontrollable antics and anguish. It reads as something that happened, although we know as human beings that the suffering all around was unbearable. Yet, they endured.

When I go through my light and momentary afflictions on earth, I think about the taunting that He endured from the spectators on the cross; the pain in His hands and feet as they were forcibly attached to the cross with those huge nails; the thought of the holes in his hands and feet tearing more and more as the hours lingered on bring me comfort as I'm enduring life's overwhelmingly painful challenges. He did it all for me. Therefore, I can hold out and wait on Him to deliver me and my family. Resurrection is surely coming after a while.

Jesus put his flesh to death in order to show us how it's done. He gave us the best examples of love, forgiveness, and dying. The greatest part of following His instructions is the resurrection that comes on the other side of the cross. After the revelation of Jesus Christ in my own life, I've experienced things that I've had to practice what He showed me is possible. In that process, I've learned that the word of God pans out fully when we follow His instructions. I'd like to share with you a few examples of how the whole process worked for me. Here's the short version of details that will be explained in more details in a later chapter of the book:

After giving me a beautiful home, the Lord instructed me to follow Matthew 6:33 "Seek ye first, the kingdom of God and His righteousness and everything else will be added to you. When my employer closed His business, the Lord told me not to take another job. For months, we laid in the anguish of losing everything. All of this was because I decided to put the will of God above my own. We were repeatedly told to find another place to live. Our car payments became severely delinquent all because I gave adherence to seek first the kingdom of God. Our electricity was disconnected for about 24 hours and the Lord came to the rescue. I was going from food pantry to food pantry to make sure that we had food to eat. For many Christians that would have been too far to go to follow God's instructions. Yet, there was such a valuable exchange for obedience to God during that time. I share it later in the book.

1) Seeing my job as my source was at issue with God. He wanted me to know that I could rely on Him. I had to crucify the job as the idol in my life. My flesh suffered as a result of it. The

mental anguish of losing everything taunted me every day, but the Lord came through for us.

2) My relationships with people were put under a microscope. God was concerned about my willingness to leave people behind in order to follow His instructions. In different scenarios, I could hear Him telling me to put Him above family, friends, and church. At points where I was unwilling, He would allow me to see disfunctions in those relationships so that I would understand that His preeminence is foundational.

3) It took me decades to find a church to fellowship with. After finding my church, God challenged me to not walk in disobedience to Him in order to fulfill the obligation of "brick and mortar". He taught me to fully follow the instruction of His voice even if it meant that church people would talk about me and not understand my purpose. In that process, I had to die to my own reputation and what people thought and said. I had to be willing to hang on the cross like He did while they mocked my name, knowing that resurrection was coming in three days.

4) My time during the day was consumed with things to do. All of which were very important. Since obedience was His goal for me, He told me to spend my time with Him in a particular way. Running errands while talking to Him was not what He had in mind. He wanted me to be still. This was so not ordinary for me. It was an extraordinary challenge because I had responsibilities. I spent hours, days, and weeks in His presence, rarely taking a break. He began to show up for me in measurable ways when I obeyed His command to do this.

At times, I still hear Him ordering me back into His presence. It is a discipline. Our every action during the day should be what He instructs us to do.
[19] Jesus gave them this answer: "Very truly I tell you, the Son can do nothing by himself; he can do only what he sees his Father doing, because whatever the Father does the Son also does. John 5:19-20

[28] *So Jesus said, "When you have lifted up[a] the Son of Man, then you will know that I am he and that I do nothing on my own but speak just what the Father has taught me. John 8:28*

I Must Decrease

The Lord is my shepherd; I shall not want.
[2] *He maketh me to lie down in green pastures: he leadeth me beside the still waters.*
[3] *He restoreth my soul: he leadeth me in the paths of righteousness for his name's sake.*
[4] *Yea, though I walk through the valley of the shadow of death, I will fear no evil: for thou art with me; thy rod and thy staff they comfort me.*
[5] *Thou preparest a table before me in the presence of mine enemies: thou anointest my head with oil; my cup runneth over.*
[6] *Surely goodness and mercy shall follow me all the days of my life: and I will dwell in the house of the Lord forever.*

As if His first appearance wasn't enough, King Jesus decided that I needed another awakening to open my eyes even the more.

It happened again. On March 25th, 2019, I sat at my desk working when I began to sense that same sense of awe. My mind started racing, but almost immediately I knew. He had returned. I didn't move at all. I just stayed as still as I could as His presence increased. In a very gentle way I heard Him say these words, "There's nothing that I cannot do. As quickly as He came, He left. Still unsure why He chose *those words* to say to me, I continue to move on in life with His purpose for my life in my heart.

A couple of weeks later, as I recall it, was a night in the month of May that as I slept, I dreamt that I was in a foreign country that I won't name, but I knew where I was. The color royal blue was exceptionally prominent in this dream. It was a beautiful color. Somehow, I was flying through the air and came down to land on the ground. This woman beckoned me to come to her. She said "Over here, we have the mark of the beast." She showed me what looked like a dresser drawer with fancy handles. The curvature of the handle was the mark. As I was whisked into the air again, I could hear the Lord say, "You've gotten separated from your group. You're going to need the Holy Spirit to meet your departure on time. Off into the air I went.

I awakened from that dream with a sense of direction. I knew what I was supposed to do. I had to acquaint myself with the Holy Spirit in a new way. I felt a sense of dependence upon Him like never before. I sought to know Him deeply. I would spend days and hours in His presence just waiting for His instruction. I knew that I could not move without Him lest I lose my way again. I embraced Him as an actual person of the godhead. Unlike before, when He was abstract and aloof, now, I treated Him like I could see Him, like He mattered. I could instantly sense His pleasure at my direct acknowledgment of Him. It was new for me. I'd previously treated Him as an appendage to the Father, and the Son. That dream brought the reality of His importance to me into clarity. I listened to the audiobook of Benny Hinn's "Good Morning Holy Spirit" repeatedly night after night. It imparted something that I didn't know was possible into my spirit. The presence of the Holy Ghost was clearly manifested in my life at that point.

From then, I understood that my spiritual ears had to be open to hear the voice of the Spirit. The Holy Spirit constantly guides us into the places, spaces, situations, and encounters that He wants us to have. On the contrary, we consistently and persistently have opposition to drown out the voice of the Spirit. It is because of the blaring noise from the world and our human interactions that it is imperative to carve out time and space for our personal fellowship with Christ. Our daily devotional and reveling in the Spirit gives us the wherewithal to conquer on the levels that God has ordained for us to excel.

In our fellowship with Christ we are literally soaking in the invisible, supernatural, yoke-destroying power of God. We are being fitted with an armored suit of the anointing. We are absorbing the essence of Christ and all of the power that He displayed and walked in down here on earth. With all of that comes the New Testament Acts of the Apostles. We currently don't see the manifestation of the power of God as seen in the New Testament because those whom He has called have not broken away from the busyness of this 21st century world in order to bask in the presence of the Lord to garner His person and power. Yes, I have been just as guilty as the next saint, which is why He chose to appear to me.

In addition to being busy, I had a plethora of personality quirks that I couldn't seem to get past that served as great excuses to ignore the calling of the Lord to obedience. Over the years, I'd heard Him give me countless instructions without them ever being more than a fleeting thought, a suggestion. God does not give suggestions. He gives instructions. Nevertheless, my many reasons for not following His instructions kept me bound in disobedience. Nearly all of my reasons were deeply rooted in my personality and it took more courage than I had to overcome them. I suffered under the bondage to these things. Over the years, I could hear the Lord talking to me about them, but my reasoning for summoning the courage was not stronger than my reasoning to continue in the bondage. It's very possible that you suffer with some of these things as well. When I say as the subtitle of this book that "I" must decrease, I'm speaking about these bondages that are intricately woven into my nature that all begin with the letter "I", introvert, intimidated, inferior, infuriated, and idolatrous. When John the Baptist said He must increase and I must decrease, He was speaking about the will of the Father in the person of Jesus Christ juxtaposed to the will of John and what his desire would have been. We would all love to be able to stay the same, accomplish the Lord's will, and have a happy ending. That's not exactly the way that it went for John and the Lord expects us to be willing to give up our will in order to accomplish His will.

This meant that all of the little eccentricities that kept me from stepping out because I might look like an oddball if I followed the Lord's will had to be sacrificed. I could not hold on to the shy five-year-old little girl who hid behind her mother, holding on to her pants leg, while she talked to friends. I had to grow up into the young lady who knew that people would probably talk about her, and be willing to step out front in the name of Jesus and say what He wanted me to say. The "I's" in my life and your life make up the essence of who we are. Is there any part of you that interferes when the voice of the Holy Spirit calls for obedience and says, 'but I can't because I…" The end of that sentence for me was "I can't because I'm too shy (I don't stand in front of people); or "I can't because I'm too inferior (these people are all more qualified than me); or maybe yours is "I can't because I'm afraid (intimidated by a person or situation); or another one of yours might be "I can't because I'm infuriated (can't forgive, can't apologize, can't love,). All of these "I's" and many more have kept me from walking in obedience. Let's take a closer look:

1.

Introvert

Bashful, sticks out to me as the descriptive verbiage that clung to me like I was wearing a polyester skirt with no slip and nylon pantyhose. I just couldn't get away from it. From as early as five years old, I can remember that's what they called me. Somehow, I associate this bashfulness with the car accident that I had when I was just five years old. I was hit by a car while crossing the street on skates. I was going to the candy lady's house crossing a small street in front of my Aunt Kitty's house. While attempting to cross a boy named "Doobie" came up behind me and pushed me down in the street. Mr. Don's car came speeding around the corner too quickly for me to get up. I personally remember nothing of this accident, but several family members confirmed that miraculously a neighborhood guy ran over to the car and picked it up and got me from under the car. Even back then, God was making sure that nothing interfered with His plan for my life. Nevertheless, I was left with a huge scar on my left arm from the accident and numerous plastic surgeries that I had over several summers of my pre-teen years.

The car accident and the scar afforded me loads of unwanted attention as a little girl. I often hid behind my mother so that no one could see me or my scar. All of the adults asked me everywhere that I went, "How's your arm?" The attention was too much. I didn't want people knowing anything about me that made me any different than anyone else. I found myself hiding from the possibility of being noticed. Today, I still run from the spotlight. I've always been incredibly fearful of being out front until recent years. The is one of the lasting strongholds that I've been instructed that I must be loosed from in the death process. That was huge for me.

I think that my bashfulness comes in part from the fear of rejection from the other children. From time to time they would laugh or joke me about my scars. I don't remember specific instances, but I do remember hiding my arm so that other children wouldn't be able to see it. I feared that they would think that I was not worthy of friendship because of it. This fear kept me shying away from any and every kind of limelight.

Rejection is painful, particularly as a child. You don't really have the wherewithal to process the emotions surrounding why you're being rejected. The critical thinking needed to separate other people's need to feel superior by rejecting you versus whether you actually deserve the rejection for something that you've done is not fully developed until later in life. No one ever explained to me that I hadn't done anything to deserve the rejection associated with my scars. I guess they just assumed that I would know that. I was only five years old though. Consequently, I've carried that fear of rejection for a large part of my life. I've shied away from social circles where I would not be clearly celebrated. If there was a chance that the people in the room would be snooty, judgmental, or harsh, I've generally avoided those circles, primarily because of this.

I have never been able to confidently walk into a room with my head held high with an assurance that I was of significant enough value amongst the group of people who were in the room. I've always walked with an awkwardness of uncertainty about who I am as a whole. Although I am sure about who I am internally, I've never known that I would or could adequately project that externally. It is for this reason that I have not walked into a number of rooms in which I probably could have dominated. That's the cost of disobedience.

This kind of disobedience is the same thing that haunted the wicked and lazy servant in Matthew 25:14-29 in The Parable of the Talents. Read it again. Someone could be completely gifted in an area with all of the backing of heaven, and yet be locked in bondage to fear. There are a thousand things to be afraid of when launching out in an area. Yet, you will never live a fulfilled life if you don't step across the threshold of what frightens you. You really have nothing but pride to lose.

An example of this is best seen in how long it took me to answer the call of God to preach. I had a very strong sense that He was calling me when the Holy Spirit took over at times when I stood to speak. The idea of people judging me or God's ability to use me was not appealing to me. Our process for entering the ministry is for the person who is called to stand and preach a *"trial"* sermon. It seemed as if I would be on trial. I could picture myself falling apart. I was very much afraid of the entire process. Remember too that I was petrified of being in the spotlight.

Eventually, the Lord clamped down on me by telling me that I was holding the truth in unrighteousness as Paul stated in Romans Chapter 1:18. I was borderline reprobate in my mind by the time that I answered the call of God. The entire first chapter of Romans spoke volumes to me. Paul said "For I am not ashamed of the gospel of Jesus Christ for it is the power of God unto salvation." Paul seemed to be able to declare the gospel in any situation which is something that I simply wasn't able to do at that time. He talks about God's punishment for those who do not worship God as God, but instead worship men, the creation, instead of the creator. By concerning myself with my "performance" in front of men, I was ascribing worship to their opinions rather than obeying God. The consequences spoken of in that chapter are very serious. I allowed Satan to challenge my willingness to give God my all. I hated the challenge and over time was able to break free, but the cost of simple disobedience was extraordinary. I knew the truth, but refused to speak it openly as God had called me to do.

[18] For the wrath of God is revealed from heaven against all ungodliness and unrighteousness of men, who hold the truth in unrighteousness; Romans 1:18

2. Intimidation

intimidate
verb
1. frighten or overawe (someone), especially in order to make them do what one wants.

Intimidation was also affirmed as a major part of who I was until recently. I had allowed everything from people, to bills, to life situations, to intimidate (frighten) me. It wasn't an easy life, but for almost fifty years, I found it easier to allow intimidation to rule me rather than to walk with the courageous posture that the Lord commanded me to walk. Finding a work around, when God wanted me to find my courage in Christ, kept me bottled up for years. I didn't actually realize that it would hinder me as much as it has. I didn't know how much courage it takes to be great.

I could look at other people and perceive that there was an element of greatness on their lives, but I'd never considered that all of the turmoil in my life was producing greatness in me. The biggest challenge for me has been overcoming the spirit of intimidation. I suspect that intimidation is a major tool in Satan's arsenal. Who will you and I be when this fear is gone?

The Bible talks a lot about boldness. I'm having to put myself in the place of some of our favorite biblical characters in order to get a real glimpse of how to overcome my own intimidation and translate their stories into my modern-day situations. Joshua could have been too intimidated to take over the leadership of the exodus of the children of Israel after the death of Moses. In Joshua Chapter 1, the Lord told Joshua to be strong and very courageous numerous times. This chapter is so powerful for understanding how God expects us to approach His assignments for us. God made GREAT promises to Joshua as He does to us, but we must ask ourselves are we moving with the instructions that God gave to Joshua. Let's take a look at it:

Joshua 1

King James Version

1 Now after the death of Moses the servant of the LORD it came to pass, that the LORD spake unto Joshua the son of Nun, Moses' minister, saying,

2 Moses my servant is dead; now therefore arise, go over this Jordan, thou, and all this people, unto the land which I do give to them, even to the children of Israel.

3 Every place that the sole of your foot shall tread upon, that have I given unto you, as I said unto Moses.

4 From the wilderness and this Lebanon even unto the great river, the river Euphrates, all the land of the Hittites, and unto the great sea toward the going down of the sun, shall be your coast.

5 There shall not any man be able to stand before thee all the days of thy life: as I was with Moses, so I will be with thee: I will not fail thee, nor forsake thee.

6 **Be strong and of a good courage**: for unto this people shalt thou divide for an inheritance the land, which I sware unto their fathers to give them.

7 Only **be thou strong and very courageous**, that thou mayest observe to do according to all the law, which Moses my servant commanded thee: turn not from it to the right hand or to the left, that thou mayest prosper withersoever thou goest.

[8] This book of the law shall not depart out of thy mouth; but thou shalt meditate therein day and night, that thou mayest observe to do according to all that is written therein: for then thou shalt make thy way prosperous, and then thou shalt have good success.
[9] Have not I commanded thee? **Be strong and of a good courage**;
be not afraid, neither be thou dismayed: for the LORD thy God is with thee whithersoever thou goest.

Now look at Joshua's response to God's command. He wasted no time moving forward. This is obedience.

[10] Then Joshua commanded the officers of the people, saying,
[11] Pass through the host, and command the people, saying, Prepare you victuals; for within three days ye shall pass over this Jordan, to go in to possess the land, which the LORD your God giveth you to possess it.

Now look at the people's response to Joshua. They jumped fully on board with the instructions that God had given Joshua. There was no reluctance or hesitation on the part of the people.

[16] And they answered Joshua, saying, All that thou commandest us we will do, and whithersoever thou sendest us, we will go.
[17] According as we hearkened unto Moses in all things, so will we hearken unto thee: only the LORD thy God be with thee, as he was with Moses.
[18] Whosoever he be that doth rebel against thy commandment, and will not hearken unto thy words in all that thou commandest him, he shall be put to death: only be strong and of a good courage.

This group was ready. They were willing to put to death anyone who was not willing to follow the instructions that God had given Joshua. This is something that we don't easily see in today's church. We don't see enough pastors who follow God's instructions the way that God issues them. We also don't have enough branches of the body to agree with the instructions that God gives to His leaders. It is because of this that we have a church that cannot meet the mandate that God has given the church in this hour.

Intimidation was a part of my natural life before I got saved; but over the years, I've seen it used in pulpits across nation. It was something that I couldn't seem to wrap my head around until I began to ask God very serious questions. What is this that I'm seeing? Why is this message coming across this way? Is this you speaking? If not, what do you want to me to do about what I'm hearing? I found my own self unable to follow the instructions of leaders because the leaders were so concerned with pleasing the people and not God. They wanted to spare the people as Moses did, which ultimately led to Moses' downfall, instead of moving in the spirit of Joshua to follow God's instructions because they were God's instructions.

If you read the account of Moses' calling in Exodus Chapters 3 and 4, you'll see that Moses had a number of insecurities that He presented to God as his reasons for not obeying what the Lord had called him to do. He asked God, "But, who should I tell them sent me? But, what if they don't believe that you spoke to me?" He said, "I can't really talk that well. I stutter. What about that?" Moses gave God all of these excuses because the task before him was intimidating. Finally, God got angry with Moses and agreed to allow Aaron, Moses' brother to go along with him to speak for Moses.

Over the years of being in the wilderness with the complaining children of Israel, Moses became frustrated because they asked for water. Although God had done many miracles already, Moses' aggravation with them mounted. God instructed Moses to speak to the rock and the water would come out, but instead Moses smote the rock. Here's what happened in Number 20:10-12:

10 Then Moses and Aaron gathered the assembly together before the rock, and he said to them, "Hear now, you rebels: shall we bring water for you out of this rock?" 11 And Moses lifted up his hand and struck the rock with his staff twice, and water came out abundantly, and the congregation drank, and their livestock. [12] *And the* LORD *said to Moses and Aaron, "Because you did not believe in me, to uphold me as holy in the eyes of the people of Israel, therefore you shall not bring this assembly into the land that I have given them."*

This is very much like the intimidation that we see happening in today's churches. We have pastors who walk in disobedience to God themselves, as Moses did in this instance. God told Moses to speak to the rock, but Moses hit the rock. Moses was a great man, as are many of our pastors, but their disobedience to God has crucified Christ afresh. In their frustrations, they use intimidation to get the message of God across to the people of God. That is far from the will of God. It leaves the congregation walking after the intimidation of men instead of in the fear of the Lord. This is critical to understanding the impairment of the church at this moment in history. The construct of the church is not what God called for in the scriptures. It falls after the orders given by men. As a result, we have a body of believers who do not reverence God, but fear pastors and leaders.

My ability to obey God had been obstructed by the disobedience of men. I didn't understand God's instructions during those periods because I had been taught to submit to the pastor at all costs. I was too afraid of making a wrong move so I did nothing. I had been momentarily neutralized by Satan's tactics. Looking back, I see that people were the primary sources for my encounters with intimidation. Ephesians 6:12 says "We wrestle not against flesh and blood, but against principalities, powers, and rulers of the darkness of this age." Every demonic encounter was leveled to silence my voice. And it worked. I didn't have the courage to speak up about any of the major things that God expected me to confront in my personal or ministry life. This produced a sense of failure and not many major accomplishments. One thing that I held tightly to was prayer. That kept me in the fight. By all accounts it looked like I was losing, but the fact that I was still in the fight was a victory of sorts.
Death to intimidation

3.

Inferiority

I My inferiority came out of ignorance. There were so many things that I simply didn't know or understand. I didn't understand people or the way that the world operates. We would see numerous young preachers climb from the debts of obscurity into the glorious limelight of ministry with seemingly effortlessness. We knew that we were called. We knew that God had a great plan for our lives, but we couldn't figure out how to survive from one day to the next. It was the constant struggle that reinforced the feeling of living on the bottom. If it were possible for God's people to be on the bottom, we were on the bottom of that group. It was incredibly painful. Our hope was rapidly fading.

The only solution for that was to keep living. In the meantime, we were failing on a regular basis. Every day was a disappointment of some sort. I couldn't understand why the Bible told me that God would supply all of my needs, but I was so broke. We couldn't pay our utility bills for months at a time. How was that possible? In my mind, we had to have been a dismal disappointment to God. That was the worst part.

Inferiority is a condition of the mind. It is a spirit that must not be tolerated. Over the years the Lord assured me that I could not be used to my fullest potential with that spirit lingering in my life. Every time that I met new people, I would automatically move to the background because I was afraid of being rejected. I was afraid that people would see that I wasn't as good as they were so I would take myself out as a contender. It wasn't that I was looking to be better, but I'd found that people seemed to like competing when that was not on my agenda. I didn't like the contention of jocking for positions so I would disappear. This happened until it was such a habit for me that it was automatic. I found God being displeased because there were circles where He needed me to be, but I bailed on Him. I was awkwardly inferior. I could sense the disfunction. I was broken from the inside.

How was I supposed to fix an internal break? I didn't think that I could do it. What I needed to understand was that despite the resounding reinforcement from my circumstances, I was not inferior. What I needed to understand was that Satan builds a case against believers. My preexisting bashfulness that was linked to my childhood was the brooding ground for a great case for Satan. Adding to my juvenile rejection, Satan used my ignorance about life, finances, ministry, and people to convince me that my circumstances were reaffirming the lack of value in me as a person and my low place on the totem pole. It was a tool that allowed access to my thought life.

If I was going to win that fight, I had to know what God said me. I had to know that God cares deeply for me. I had to know that there's not something wrong with me when things go wrong other than a simple lack of understanding. I had to know that God was not plotting against me because He thought that I was a bad person. I needed Jeremiah 29:11 "For I know the plans that I have for you, declares the Lord, plans to prosper you and not to harm you, to give you a hope and a future." I needed to believe that in every situation, no matter how it looked, or what the outcome of the situation was. I needed to believe it.

Additionally, there were times when people would use my insecurity as a source of gratification for their own personality quirks. The cruelty, the manipulation, and the lack of love that other people walked in initially served as a reinforcement for the inferiority that I felt. It was hard for me to acknowledge and accept the cruelty of people because I don't function that way. I hadn't come to the realization that as Jesus stated in John 15:25 "they hated me without a cause." I couldn't imagine that people would be so spiteful for no good reason. Consequently, I took their disfunction as my own and internalized their misery into my inferiority. I've learned that I can't always be the one to fall on the sword and say "I'm the weird one." Sometimes we run into cases where they're the weird ones. We should learn from those cases and move on. Over the years, I allowed inferiority to consume me.

I was so self-absorbed in my own insecurities that I couldn't get past Go.
"I will praise thee; for I am fearfully and wonderful made: marvelous are thy works; and that my soul knoweth right well. Psalms 139:14

4.

Infuriated

Anger was my go to emotion. Although it only escaped my lips on occasions of marked challenges, I've lived with it embodying my soul for very long periods of time throughout the years. Going through offenses regularly, challenged me. The limits of my love have been tested repeatedly in many ways. I found that people took my meekness for weakness, consequently pushing me far beyond the limitations that I was comfortable with. Those times produced set it off moments. I have never really been hotheaded, but being pushed over a period of time allowed anger and resentment to fester. Hoping and praying that the offenders would see the light proved to be unfruitful in the timeframes where my emotions were abated. Continued relationships with those people offered more opportunities to be mishandled. After years and years of relationships with people, mostly family, who appeared to be unchanged, I finally went KABOOM! My husband affectionately called me Katie Kaboom for a few years in the early 2000's. I wasn't interested in being anyone's doormat. My profession of Christianity forced me to have to figure out how to handle my anger in a godly way.

On too many occasions I've found myself seething after an incident of pure putridness. This uncontrollable anger branched out from the root of my father. While I've seen his anger in glimpses of fury throughout my life when my sisters, my mother, or I had done something unconscionable in his mind, my own anger seemed to be worse. That's because it was inside of *me*. Katie Kaboom's explosions made perfect sense in her teenage world, but her family tiptoed around her to keep from upsetting her. She was a teenager, but I was in my thirties. ***Disclaimer: It's***

in your 20's and 30's that you learn exactly how cruel the world can be.

My husband would often remind me that anger is a secondary emotion. With that understanding, I took to unravel what was my primary emotion. The intensity of my anger didn't make it primary. It was secondary because there was another emotion fueling it. That emotion was fear. I was terrified of so many things over the years. I was afraid of rejection in my early years. I was afraid of not being good enough in my early twenties. I was afraid of the world and all of the dangers of it in my late twenties. I was afraid that we wouldn't be able to take care of our children in my thirties. I was afraid that we would never recover from our church failures in my thirties. I was afraid that I would never be able to devote my life to what I love doing, being a creative, in my thirties and forties. I was afraid that we would never get out of poverty in my late thirties and forties. I was afraid that we would never find a decent pastor in my forties. I was afraid that my children wouldn't recover from their childhood failures in my mid-forties. I was afraid that my marriage wouldn't last in my late forties and so on.

As you can see, every given topic was draped in fear. The fear produced a feeling of powerlessness, which moved into having a form of godliness, but denying the power thereof. The absence of the gospel being preached with power to empower left me powerless. I couldn't rely on a preacher, I had to rely on the Holy Spirit as previously stated. The scripture confirms it in 1 John 2:27 "[27] *But the anointing which ye have received of him abideth in you, and ye need not that any man teach you: but as the same anointing teacheth you of all things, and is truth, and is no lie, and even as it hath taught you, ye shall abide in him.*

It is entirely possible to live at peace. We simply have to get to the core of our emotions and draw the boundaries of our lives accordingly. If we're serious about walking with God, anger will not remain our go to emotion. The scripture says *"Follow peace with all men, and holiness, without which no man shall see the Lord. Looking diligently lest any man fail of the grace of God; lest any root of bitterness springing up trouble you, and thereby many be defiled Hebrews 12:14-15.*

5.

Idolatrous

This was huge for me. I had so many idols, even though I professed to be a Christian. I really had no idea of how I could open the door and invite so many idols into my life. In very simple terms, it comes from not putting God first. He is and always should be preeminent in our lives. God is the source of everything for us. Anything that we look to as our source can be defined as an idol. Jobs, spouses, children, banks, money, material possessions, churches, political organizations, education, and so on can be considered idols if we look to those things as our source for life, movement, or existence. *28 For in him we live, and move, and have our being; as certain also of your own poets have said, For we are also his offspring. Acts 17:28*

If our life does not flow out of Him, it flows out of something else. That's an idol. God cannot be replaced, nor should we ever want to substitute Him with anything else. Every day, the Holy Spirit should have free reign to dictate the comings and goings of our lives. If our spouses or children are occupying that space, we have given them the influence and dictate that God desires to have in our lives. If our jobs tell us whether or not we can attend church on Sunday, we have replaced God with our employer. If the bank tells us whether or not we can purchase a home, we have bowed to the banking system. If our finances tell us whether or not we can take a vacation, we have yielded to the almighty dollar.

There are numerous resources that God can use to funnel His blessings to us. We simply cannot rely on the funnel. It's just a mechanism of transportation from the source. It's not actually the source. We sometimes see African women on television carrying jugs of water that they have filled from the river fifty miles away. Then, we'll see the same woman rejoicing because a missionary has drilled a well deep enough in her village to tap the water from the same river. It's the same water coming from the same river. The mechanism of transportation, however, has changed.

The source of a thing is its place of origin. The river is the source of the water. How it gets to the village is an entirely different thing. We should never place our confidence in the vehicle, but always understand that the point of origin is what we need to stay connected with. *Psalms 100:3 says Know ye that the LORD he is God: it is he that hath made us, and not we ourselves; we are his people, and the sheep of his pasture. Enter into His gates with thanksgiving and into His courts with praise.* It's telling us to acknowledge God as the source of life for us and rejoice in it. Give Him the praise and acknowledgement that He is rightfully due.

What we do instead is to heap up all kinds of lusts and desires that are fed to us from the world. We allow the lust of the flesh, the lust of the eye, and the pride of life to override our faithfulness to our creator. Our hearts should long for the opportunity to exalt Him in our lives. Our daily surrender is the only thing that can allow that opportunity to come forth in our lives.

I want to share with you that one source of the primary idols in my life was various church leaders whom I trusted to give wise counsel and direction. The great challenge therein is that at times God will give us personal instructions that our leaders are not able to see because of a variety of issues. There are times when the spiritual training of our leaders is not consistent with the scriptures; and they will hold to those teachings rather than lean on what the scripture says. Because God does not change, He's going to instruct you in line with what His word says. That conflict can be tremendously challenging. Many pastors train their ministers and leaders to follow them even if they give instruction that is contrary to what the scripture says.

In 2002, we had a pastor who asked the congregation, how many people would follow him off of a cliff. He gave the story of Alexander the Great who had trained his army to do so. Almost everyone in that service raised their hands except myself and another woman. We looked at each other, shrugged our shoulders, and did a little grin to say "Ahh, No". We were friends. Later in the week we just laughed about it because we knew there was no way that we would do that. Unfortunately, that's how many pastors teach their people. And yes, there are numerous congregations who are all in for it. Following a pastor off of a cliff is entirely different than following God off of a cliff.

God has made it exceptionally clear to me over the years that our pastors are fallible. We must maintain our focus on Him because He will never lead us in the wrong direction. Every pastor that we've had has walked in the flesh at some point. We're still in our human bodies so it's difficult for them to never have a moment where their humanity overrides their divinity. Yet, many of our pastors denied their fallibility. We were never initially nitpicky in our approach to leadership. We've consistently been excessively tolerant, only to have leaders turn and throw javelins as we sat playing our harps. Even more specifically many leaders have succumbed to the control of Jezebel. They walk in the spirit of Ahab and find it outrageously offensive when, in the spirit of Elijah and Jehu, we walk in our God-given authority as believers.

Consequently, in over thirty years of ministry, Isaiah 6:1-8 has been profoundly relevant in our lives. This is where we have lived much of our spiritual existence from:

***6** In the year that king Uzziah died I saw also the Lord sitting upon a throne, high and lifted up, and his train filled the temple.*
2 Above it stood the seraphims: each one had six wings; with twain he covered his face, and with twain he covered his feet, and with twain he did fly.
3 And one cried unto another, and said, Holy, holy, holy, is the Lord of hosts: the whole earth is full of his glory.

4 And the posts of the door moved at the voice of him that cried,
and the house was filled with smoke.
5 Then said I, Woe is me! for I am undone; because I am a man of
unclean lips, and I dwell in the midst of a people of unclean lips:
for mine eyes have seen the King, the Lord of hosts.
6 Then flew one of the seraphims unto me, having a live coal in his
hand, which he had taken with the tongs from off the altar:
7 And he laid it upon my mouth, and said, Lo, this hath touched thy
lips; and thine iniquity is taken away, and thy sin purged.
8 Also I heard the voice of the Lord, saying, Whom shall I send,
and who will go for us? Then said I, Here am I; send me.

I've only shared with you a few of the "I's" that the Lord shared with me. There are several more that I went through getting rid of in the dying process. These "I's" made up the things that were standing in the way of obedience to Christ in my life. Together they were linked to form a stronghold of bondage. As I wrestled with each of them, the stronghold became weaker. I began to feel my freedom returning to me.

Your I's will make up who you are. Don't be afraid to be honest with yourself. When we recognized our I's, they can no longer hinder us from being obedient to God.

OBEDIENCE

compliance with an order, request, or law or submission to another's authority

A man named Christopher was walking along a steep cliff one day when he accidentally got too close to the edge and fell. On the way down he grabbed a branch, which temporarily stopped his fall. He looked down and to his horror saw that the canyon fell straight down for more than a thousand feet. He couldn't hang onto the branch forever, and there was no way for him to climb up the steep wall of the cliff.

So, Chris began yelling for help, hoping that someone passing by would hear him and lower a rope or something. "HELP! HELP! Is

anyone up there? "HELP!" He yelled for a long time, but no one heard him. He was about to give up when he heard a voice.
"Chris, Chris. Can you hear me?"
"Yes, yes! I can hear you. I'm down here!"
"I can see you, Chris. Are you all right?"
"Yes, but who are you, and where are you?
"I am the Lord, Chris. I'm everywhere."
"The Lord? You mean, GOD?"
"That's Me."
"God, please help me! I promise if, you'll get me down from here, I'll stop sinning. I'll be a really good person. I'll serve You for the rest of my life."
"Easy on the promises, Chris. Let's get you off from there, then we can talk."
"Now, here's what I want you to do. Listen carefully."
"I'll do anything, Lord. Just tell me what to do."
"Okay. Let go of the branch."
"What?"
"I said, let go of the branch." Just trust Me. Let go."
There was a long silence.
Finally Chris yelled, "HELP! HELP! IS ANYONE ELSE UP THERE?"

There are a few challenging commands that Jesus gives. Our willingness to do them requires death to our own will and flesh. Our souls and bodies must align with the Spirit of God that lives in our human spirit. In order for the redemptive value of our purchased lives to be manifested, the three must agree as one. Just as the Father, son, and Holy Spirit are a triune being and all agree as one, we too are a triune being, spirit, soul, and body that must agree as one. Here's where Roman 12:1-2 come in:

***12** I beseech you therefore, brethren, by the mercies of God, that ye present your bodies a living sacrifice, holy, acceptable unto God, which is your reasonable service.*

2 And be not conformed to this world, but be ye transformed by the renewing of your mind, that ye may prove what is that good and acceptable and perfect will of God.

Paul says this is what must be done in order for the perfect will of God to come forth.

Here are some of the commandments that Jesus gave us that we must obey in order to accomplish His will:

Surrender

James 4:7 Submit yourselves therefore to God. Resist the devil, and he will flee from you.

Surrendering is an admission to giving up. What would we be giving up on? Giving up on having the answers, giving up on knowing it all, giving up on being the smartest one in the room, giving up on pushing our own agenda. God the Father is always in pursuit of His children. He passionately chases us in an effort to overwhelm us with His love. Our surrender is a relenting to the obsessive pursuit of the King. We're saying "Okay God, you can have me. You can have your way."

Sometimes pain causes us to build up the walls of our defenses in order to keep going. Our surrender acknowledges that not even the internal barriers of protection that we have constructed can save us.

Love

12This is My commandment, that you love one another as I have loved you. 13
Greater love hath no man than this, that a man lay down his life for his friends.

While love is mischaracterized by Hollywood as a euphoric emotion that accompanies a myriad of relational possibilities, it too is challenging in the midst of a fallen world. With demonic forces making daily presentations to get us off of our love game, it takes a concerted effort to maintain the love. One of the primary scriptures that I focus on these days is the one that says, "**12** And because iniquity shall abound, the love of many shall wax cold." Jesus is sharing with the disciples in Matthew 25 what will happen in the last days. That's where he shares this verse. We have certainly reached those days in today's world. That abundance of hatred that is running through the streets can be overwhelming. I've found myself internalizing the hatred. It hurts. It's painful, and yet Jesus tells us to love our enemies.

Remembering what we've been taught has to take priority in these times. These days are requiring us to dig deeper and deeper into the scriptures in order to understand the love of God. The complexity of yielding even to the point of physical death could be what Christians could someday face. The mental preparation for that possibility goes beyond the Sunday School version of Jesus' death on the cross. The deep psychological preparation and willingness to surrender all is what Jesus is telling us that we need in order to be who He has called us to be. There is an abundance of hatred swirling around in the world's atmosphere. The only thing that can help us to overcome it is the real, genuine love that Christ showed us in His death.

Forgive

24Therefore I say unto you, What things soever ye desire, when ye pray, believe that ye receive them, and ye shall have them. 25And when ye stand praying, forgive, if ye have ought against any: that your Father also which is in heaven may forgive you your trespasses. 26But if ye do not forgive, neither will your Father which is in heaven forgive your trespasses.

Sometimes forgiving people is the hardest thing to do. It hurts when people that you love willfully do things that tear your heart to pieces. The hatred that other people level towards you makes forgiveness by far one of the greatest challenges of our Christian lives. Yet, Jesus so readily did it on the cross for us. My heart yearns to understand exactly what was in His mind that helped Him to be able to do that. I haven't had anyone do anything nearly as brutal to me as Jesus did, yet the test of forgiveness remains a challenge. Meditating on the word of God has a medicinal effect of breaking up all of the foulness that keeps us from being able to let go and forgive. Let's look in the word:

1Then said he unto the disciples, It is impossible but that offences will come: but woe unto him, through whom they come! 2It were better for him that a millstone were hanged about his neck, and he cast into the sea, than that he should offend one of these little ones. 3Take heed to yourselves: If thy brother trespass against thee, rebuke him; and if he repent, forgive him. 4And if he trespass against thee seven times in a day, and seven times in a day turn again to thee, saying, I repent; thou shalt forgive him.

Jesus is assuring the disciples that offenses will come. He compels them to forgive one another highlighting that their own forgiveness would hinge on their ability to forgive others. The disciples then tell Jesus to increase their faith. They realize that it will take faith in order to forgive like Jesus was compelling them to. They would have faith to have faith in God to settle the score of offenses. Even when people hurt us the most that has to be there response, one of faith. I heard one person describe forgiveness in this way, he asked, "Do you accept the blood of Jesus Christ as the full payment for the sin that was committed against you?" If you do, then you have to let it go understanding that their sin was paid for by Jesus on the cross. They are no longer indebted to you for their offense. That requires chewing and digesting, but it is the accurate approach to forgiveness.

Give

"Give, and it shall be given unto you; good measure, pressed down, and shaken together, and running over, shall men give into your bosom. For with the same measure that ye mete withal it shall be measured to you again."

Our giving can often be an answered prayer for the person to whom we are giving. We don't have the luxury of disobeying a command to give because we don't like the person he tells us to give to, or because we're going to be lacking in some way, or because the cost of giving is more than we want to pay. Our journey of faith should inform us that when we give there is always a reciprocal blessing on the other end of the gift. Jesus said *"Give, and it shall be given unto you; good measure, pressed down, and shaken together, and running over, shall men give into your bosom. For with the same measure that ye mete withal it shall be measured to you again."* Consequently, when we withhold from giving when the Holy Spirit has instructed us to do so, we're standing in the way of our own blessing.

Unfortunately, we don't know which blessing it is that we're passing up on. It could be the healing, financial blessing, promotion, or salvation of a loved one that we've been desperately praying for. Obedience in the area of giving can affect any number of circumstances with which we're dealing. I've followed God's instructions in this area and have reaped the rewards of it.

The Rewards for Obedience

If we suffer, we shall also reign with him: 2 Timothy 2:12

There are rewards for obedience.

In 2018, after going through yet another episode of near homelessness, we found the house that we live in today. My heart had been broken a thousand times by the devastation of one-sided circumstances. This last time, we'd been paying rent to our landlord, but he hadn't been paying his mortgage company. Without knowing it, the house that we were renting went into foreclosure. At some point, the bank began to send notices in our landlord's name to the house that we were renting. Somehow, they must have found out that we were renting it because after a while they began to send notices to both us and him. We opened the letters addressed to us just to find out that we had to move. The bank was willing to pay us to leave the house by a certain date, but for one reason or another we couldn't seem to get ourselves together to leave.

That date came around and we still hadn't found a place to live. Consequently, we spent a little over a month moving from hotel to hotel every three days. Sometimes we'd stay longer, but we could only stay as long as our money lasted. There were days when we had no money and an upcoming payment needed to be made in order to remain in the hotel. We were staying in a resort city so there were places willing to give us hotel vouchers if we'd listen to their ninety-minute spill about a timeshare. That kept us off of the street for a week. We knew that we had to find a place and quick.

I'd went to my 5 a.m. prayer meeting at my friend's church when I heard the Lord say as clear as anything that I've ever heard, "Today is your day." I knew He would give us a house on that day. We still had no money! But God had said it. All day long, as we drove around doing our daily activities, we would write down the addresses and phone numbers of places that had "For Rent" signs in the front yard. Well, it had gotten to be about 7:30 at night when we were leaving our local library. There was a sign on the main highway. We called the phone number on the sign. The owner answered the phone and answered all of the pertinent questions like "How much is the place?" and "How many bedrooms and baths?" It was within our price range and there was enough space for all of us. He told us to come over.

Ok now, who shows a property at 7:30 at night in December, but God? We drove up to the house and could hardly believe our eyes. Externally, it was an extraordinary house. It sits on the Indian River in Chesapeake, Virginia. We were dumbfounded. By the look of this house, even though we could afford it, we just knew that we'd have to pass a steep credit check. We walked through the house and talked to the owner. Boy, we loved the house. As we prepared to leave, we asked the owner could we have an application for the house. He gave us a small handwritten piece of paper, told us to fill it out and bring it back. On this paper was a space for our name, employer, and personal references. Huh? We thought to ourselves. "What is this?" It was almost inconceivable that the only information that the owners were asking for was our names, employers, and references.

We took the completed piece of paper back to the mild-mannered older couple. He asked "When would we like to move in?" We grinned and looked at each other in a way as not to seem overly excited, but internally we were doing summersaults. It was December 21st so we said after Christmas because that's when my husband would get paid again. The salt and pepper haired older gentlemen said "Why don't y'all just move in now and pay me when you get your next paycheck." That was an amazing Christmas present for our then, 16-year-old daughter who had seen quite a bit of hard knocks over the past few months. We were elated! The view from our kitchen and the two bedrooms on the back of our house is stunning. I could imagine that this was God's reward for obedience. The struggle was exceptionally real, but God had recompense on His mind. We'd never lived in a house that looked so abundant. Every time I have to give someone my address, I can't help but think about how graciously He blessed us with this beautiful place.

The story goes on just a bit further. When we brought the "application" back to the owner, my husband shared with him the story of what I'd heard from God on the morning that we'd first called him. The gentleman shared with my husband that he and his wife had been praying about to whom they should rent their house. He said that they'd seen over sixty families to no avail, but when they'd met us, his wife said "They're the ones." They had a sense of peace about renting to us even though half of our clothing was visible in our 1999 Ford Explorer. We looked like we had climbed out of a piece of luggage. We've lived in this house for two years and we're still in awe of our God. There are rewards for obedience.

The materialism that has engulfed today's preachers and Christ followers is a far cry from anything that I'd like to be associated with. My family has endured innumerable trials so to finally reach the place where you have a sense that God is truly in your corner is scrumptious. We've endured abuse of varying kinds within our family ranks; internal family fighting and turmoil, rebellion ranging from drug abuse to runaway children, lack and poverty like I'd never witnessed in my own family, repeated rejections within the church, failures in ministry and in the marketplace. The Langfords have walked through some earthly variations of hell; consequently, to have God be so sweet as to manufacture my wildest dream felt pretty good. It seemed as if we had crossed a threshold into the garden of God's blessings. It seemed to be where the beautiful things are.

We have a plethora of stories like that entailing our cars, jobs, children, college educations, etc. Allow me to give you just a few more testimonies to give you the incentive to keep reading. While, I told you how the Lord prompted me to pull away and spend time with Him in the early years, I didn't completely share all of the internal workings of why. God has given me numerous gifts, two of which are art and design. For years, I spent time being on an off of jobs because I was either pregnant and raising children or spending time trying to follow God. In those times where I was simply following God, it was not easy for me. My husband brought in all of the finances at those times. He did not understand why I wasn't helping to contribute to the house financially. The fact that most marriages end because of financial reasons wasn't much of a help either. That weighed on me heavily. At first, in the times that I did take off to follow God, I really wasn't doing it in faith because we were constantly arguing about whether or not I should be working. We had so many household questions that needed to be answered. God wasn't answering. This is a journey that is walked, by faith.

After getting positioned to be blessed by the Lord, I began to see the fruit of having a home church, having a pastor that hears from God, having unwillingness to hold on to offense, and a prayer life was that fruitful. I had a desire to walk in obedience. All of this was a part of positioning. In May 2019, my employer closed shop and I was out of a job. God instructed me in so many ways not to take another job after He'd blessed us with our beautiful house. I spent my time with Him. I shared with my grown sons that I wasn't trying to get a job because I wanted the two sons who were living at home to be able to maintain the household bills along with their father. This is what I believed needed to be done so that my sons would understand their roles when they get married and move into their own homes. I wanted them to feel the weight of it while they were still in our house and we could help out. I wanted to follow God and heed to His instructions. Without my income, our money got tight. I could hear the Lord say "I want you to sow a seed." By this time, I'd learned to hear His voice and know that it was Him. I was being bombarded daily with feelings of guilt and thoughts of "what if?" I had been in that situation multiple times before and had never seen it work out well.

There I was again following God. I was at a different stage in my life and had a different level of confidence in God. I needed to make a statement of faith. The purpose of this seed was to show Satan that no matter how much he threatened our sustainability, I still trusted God. I wasn't out on a whim on my own. I was following God's instructions. Money was not going to rule over me. Pinching pennies and holding on to every dime was not going to be how I survived because the scripture says that "Man shall not live by bread alone, but by every word that proceeded out of the mouth of God." So, if I give all of it and I'm without enough to pay my bills, I had to trust God because He said to do it. That was a pretty big leap, but not really, simply because God said to do it.

I was in the house that I loved. After being nearly homeless, I was willing to put the well-being of my new house on the line because God said to do it. Over the years, we've moved regularly every few years and not always because we were ready to go. I talked to the Lord about that. I was tired of moving. I wanted stability. "Yes, God you've always provided as you said that you would, but that didn't keep us from having to move constantly." These were my words to Him, "I've seen the God who provides, but now I want to see the God who sustains." Boy, after I prayed that prayer, my heart was so entangled with Him. This was everything. I could not take another failure. I needed Him to come through for us.

I sowed the seed in my church. Not only did God keep every bill in my house paid, but he gave every man in my house a raise.

My oldest son, got a new job making a full eight dollars per hour more than he was making. My second oldest son, who'd worked part-time at his job for the past four years, was given a promotion to full-time with increased wages. My dear husband, who had been all over the place with jobs, primarily self-employed, received a job with the city making more than he has ever made in a supervisory position for the city. In the meantime, I am able to be at home and do the things that God has called me to do, whatever they may be, just like I've always wanted. Somebody asked, "Won't He do it?' I can say, "Yes He will!"

Now, the greatest reward for obedience that I've seen to date is the resurrection life of Jesus Christ being restored to my mother. On Thanksgiving of 2019, my entire family went to my mother's house for Thanksgiving dinner even though it occurred at 12 noon. We spent time with my mother and father, and ate dinner. My husband and I and three of our kids had left to go feed the homeless with another church. We'd gotten about ten minutes up the interstate when my oldest sister called my cell phone screaming "She's gone!' I didn't know what she was talking about, but I could hear the terror in my sister's voice. I was horrified just by the screaming, but then she said "Momma's gone! She's not breathing! We've tried to wake her up, but she's not breathing!" Everything in me tried to stay calm because it just didn't seem real. We'd just left the house and she was perfectly fine. I asked my sister what happened and she said that our mother was eating and then she began to cough. She coughed a couple of times and then her head slumped over. She said that they had tried to do the Heimlich maneuver, my father even slapped her a couple of times trying to awaken her, but nothing worked. Immediately, we turned the car around and headed back towards my mother's house. My sister hung up the phone and we began to pray.

I reasoned out loud "Well, at least Mommy got to see her entire family all at once." I said that a couple of time, but it didn't seem to catch on in the spirit for me. Then something arose in me to say "But God! You're still able!" I began to make that declaration with fervor. We began to intercede for my mother and call on the Lord. I called my niece back on the phone because I wanted to see my mother. By that time the ambulance workers were there and they had already determined that they couldn't get a pulse. I asked my niece to show me my mother's face on FaceTime. My mother was slumped over in her wheelchair looking lifeless with her head hanging down over her neck. I hung up the phone with my niece and began to intercede even more. Finally, I yelled "Mother! Come back to your body!" We were still a few minutes away and continued praying.

When I got to my mother's house, I ran in the door past the emergency workers to see my mother sitting there with her beautiful eyes wide open! I gave her the biggest hug and began to rejoice without inhibition. I ran outside to yell to the world, "What a Mighty God We Serve!" It was amazing and life giving to every single member of our family. Any skeptics in the family were convinced on that day that our God reigns!

I told you, there are rewards for obedience. Our natural life is not an indication of how we are doing spiritually, but if you're a Christian, there are going to be signs that indicate that the blessing of the Lord is on your natural life. Everyone who is blessed naturally is not spiritually on point, but God blesses those who obey His voice. Don't be fooled. These testimonies do not tell you that there was a long period of disobedience in my life, even though I called myself a Christian. As my shepherd, the Lord led me down the path towards obedience.

Again, Isaiah 40:28-31 says
"Have you not known?
Have you not heard?
The everlasting God, the LORD,
The Creator of the ends of the earth,
Neither faints nor is weary.
His understanding is unsearchable.
29 He gives power to the weak,
And to *those who have* no might He increases strength.
30 Even the youths shall faint and be weary,

And the young men shall utterly fall,
31 But those who wait on the LORD
Shall renew *their* strength;
They shall mount up with wings like eagles,
They shall run and not be weary,
They shall walk and not faint.

Days of Purim

For me, no story gives more clarity to the importance and relevance of obedience in today's times than the story of Esther. The preceding incidents that laid out the necessity of Esther in the house of Ahasuerus went way back into her family's circumstance, the national standing of the Jews, and the internal making of her character. If you read the book of Esther you'll find that Esther was orphaned and being raised by her cousin Mordecai at a time when Israel was in captivity. The king had previously banished his first wife Vashti from ever being in his presence again because she refused to come to display how beautiful she was before all of the people and officials. There was a search made throughout the land for a new Queen. The most beautiful women were sought after for this prestigious purpose and platform. Mordecai, Esther's cousin entered her into the selection process and encouraged her not to share that she was a Jew. After a yearlong process of weeding through all of the other women, Esther was chosen by King Ahasuerus to be his new Queen.

In the meantime, the King also promoted Haman to be his right-hand man. He felt that the honor bestowed upon him should be that when the common folks see Haman coming through, that they would bow in honor of Him. This was good until Haman passed Mordecai, Esther's principled cousin. Mordecai refused to bow to Haman, as bowing is an act of worship in the Jewish tradition. This was an honor only to be bestowed upon the one God Jehovah that the Jews served. When Mordecai refused to bow, Haman went after his neck and those of all of the Jews. Haman went to the king to have a decree drawn up so that all Jews would be annihilated. Not knowing that his own wife was a Jew, King Ahasuerus agreed to Haman's decree. When Mordecai found out, he sat outside of the king's gate in sackcloth and ashes mourning and wailing over this decree. This is where we will pick up the story in Esther Chapter 4:

When Mordecai perceived all that was done, Mordecai rent his clothes, and put on sackcloth and ashes, and went out into the midst of the city, and cried with a loud and a bitter cry;

And came even before the king's gate: for none might enter into the king's gate clothed with sackcloth.

And in every province, whithersoever the king's commandment and his decree came, there was great mourning among the Jews, and fasting, and weeping, and wailing; and many lay in sackcloth and ashes.

4So Esther's maids and her chamberlains came and told it her.
Then was the queen exceedingly grieved; and she sent raiment to
clothe Mordecai, and to take away his sackcloth from him: but he
received it not. 5Then called Esther for Hatach, one of the king's
chamberlains, whom he had appointed to attend upon her, and
gave him a commandment to Mordecai, to know what it was, and
why it was. 6So Hatach went forth to Mordecai unto the street of
the city, which was before the king's gate. 7And Mordecai told him
of all that had happened unto him, and of the sum of the money
that Haman had promised to pay to the king's treasuries for the
Jews, to destroy them. 8Also he gave him the copy of the writing of
the decree that was given at Shushan to destroy them, to
shew it unto Esther, and to declare it unto her, and to charge her
that she should go in unto the king, to make supplication unto him,
and to make request before him for her people.

9And Hatach came and told Esther the words of Mordecai. 10Again
Esther spake unto Hatach, and gave him commandment unto
Mordecai; 11All the king's servants, and the people of the king's
provinces, do know, that whosoever, whether man or woman, shall
come unto the king into the inner court, who is not called, there
is one law of his to put him to death, except such to whom the king
shall hold out the golden sceptre, that he may live: but I have not
been called to come in unto the king these thirty days. 12And they
told to Mordecai Esther's words.

13Then Mordecai commanded to answer Esther, Think not with
thyself that thou shalt escape in the king's house, more than all the

Jews. 14For if thou altogether holdest thy peace at this time, then shall there enlargement and deliverance arise to the Jews from another place; but thou and thy father's house shall be destroyed: and who knoweth whether thou art come to the kingdom for such a time as this?

Esther's story clearly depicts God divine providence in ordering the steps of our lives. God will always raise up someone to fulfill his plan; however, the outcome that occurs for us and generations to follow are a result of our own decisions to obey or disobey God.

In this instance, as in so many that we face, the consequences either way could have been dire. At least by following God's instruction, Esther had the favor of God on her side. Any other choice, as stated in the prophetic utterance of Mordecai, would have left Esther personally on the outskirts of deliverance. As in Esther's life, sometimes we are raised to positions of prominence, not so that we can promenade through the halls of regalia, but for God's divine purposes. Sometimes the fate of a people can rest on the obedience of one.

The time of rejoicing following the deliverance of the Jews from the edict of Haman was beautifully noted in Esther 9:

The Feast of Purim Instituted
18But the Jews that were at Shushan assembled together on the thirteenth day thereof, and on the fourteenth thereof; and on the fifteenth day of the same they rested, and made it a day of feasting and gladness. 19Therefore the Jews of the villages, that dwelt in the unwalled towns, made the fourteenth day of the month Adar a day of gladness and feasting, and a good day, and of sending portions one to another.
20And Mordecai wrote these things, and sent letters unto all the Jews that were in all the provinces of the king Ahasuerus, both nigh and far, 21To stablish this among them, that they should keep the fourteenth day of the month Adar, and the fifteenth day of the same, yearly, 22As the days wherein the Jews

rested from their enemies, and the month which was turned unto
them from sorrow to joy, and from mourning into a good day: that
they should make them days of feasting and joy, and of sending
portions one to another, and gifts to the poor.
23*And the Jews undertook to do as they had begun, and as*
Mordecai had written unto them; 24*Because Haman the son of*
Hammedatha, the Agagite, the enemy of all the Jews, had devised
against the Jews to destroy them, and had cast Pur, that is, the lot,
to consume them, and to destroy them; 25*But when Esther came*
before the king, he commanded by letters that his wicked device,
which he devised against the Jews, should return upon his own
head, and that he and his sons should be hanged on the
gallows. 26*Wherefore they called these days Purim after the name*
of Pur. Therefore for all the words of this letter, and of that which
they had seen concerning this matter, and which had come unto
them, 27*The Jews ordained, and took upon them, and upon their*
seed, and upon all such as joined themselves unto them, so as it
should not fail, that they would keep these two days according to
their writing, and according to their appointed time every
year; 28*And that these days should be remembered and kept*
throughout every generation, every family, every province, and
every city; and that these days of Purim should not fail from
among the Jews, nor the memorial of them perish from their seed.
29*Then Esther the queen, the daughter of Abihail, and Mordecai*
the Jew, wrote with all authority, to confirm this second letter of
Purim. 30*And he sent the letters unto all the Jews, to the hundred*
twenty and seven provinces of the kingdom of
Ahasuerus, with words of peace and truth, 31*To confirm these*
days of Purim in their times appointed, according as Mordecai the
Jew and Esther the queen had enjoined them, and as they had
decreed for themselves and for their seed, the matters of the
fastings and their cry. 32*And the decree of Esther confirmed these*
matters of Purim; and it was written in the book.

Imagine the festivities that you will have on the day that you are delivered from your enemies!

Praise God!

Praise God!

Praise God!

My prayer in all of this is that you understand the requirement of obedience. Our salvation hangs on our obedience to God's instructions. We must take a much closer look at the actual embodiment of the gospel, not as a feel-good token, but words to live by.

The End

www.ingramcontent.com/pod-product-compliance
Ingram Content Group UK Ltd.
Pitfield, Milton Keynes, MK11 3LW, UK
UKHW020347250726
13967UKWH00005B/2163